EARTHFORMS

DUNES

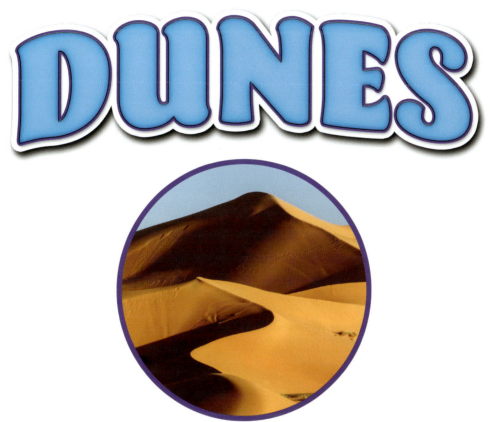

By Martha London

Consultant: Beth Gambro
Reading Specialist, Yorkville, Illinois

Minneapolis, Minnesota

Teaching Tips

Before Reading

- Look at the cover of the book. Discuss the picture and the title.
- Ask readers to brainstorm a list of what they already know about dunes. What can they expect to see in the book?
- Go on a picture walk, looking through the pictures to discuss vocabulary and make predictions about the text.

During Reading

- Read for purpose. Encourage readers to think about characteristics of dunes.
- Ask readers to look for the details of the book. Where are dunes found?
- If readers encounter an unknown word, ask them to look at the sounds in the word. Then, ask them to look at the rest of the page. Are there any clues to help them understand?

After Reading

- Encourage readers to pick a buddy and reread the book together.
- Ask readers to name two animals found near dunes. Find the pages that tell about these animals.
- Ask readers to write or draw something they learned about dunes.

Credits

Cover and title page, © cceliaphoto/Adobe Stock; 3, © zanskar/iStock; 5, © Petrichuk/iStock; 6–7, © beingbonny/iStock; 8–9, © trongnguyen/Adobe Stock; 11T, © Ghulam Hussain/iStock; 11BL, © Dmytro Kosmenko/iStock; 11BR, © Francois/Adobe Stock; 12–13, © zombiu26/Shutterstock; 15T, © Daniel Bouquets/Shutterstock; 15B, © Image Professionals GmbH / Alamy Stock Photo; 16, © Bieniecki/iStock; 17, © Steve Bower/Shutterstock; 19, © ae-photos/iStock; 21, © Mlenny/iStock; 22T, © izanbar/iStock; 22M, © fdastudillo/iStock; 22B, © Richard/Adobe Stock; 23TL, © Elena Goosen/iStock; 23TR, © the_lightwriter/Adobe Stock; 23BL, © adamkaz/iStock; 23B © Jef Wodniack/iStock.

See BearportPublishing.com for our statement on Generative AI Usage.

Library of Congress Cataloging-in-Publication Data

Names: London, Martha, author.
Title: Dunes / by Martha London ; Consultant: Beth Gambro, Reading
   Specialist, Yorkville Illinois.
Description: Bearcub books. | Minneapolis, Minnesota : Bearport Publishing
   Company, [2025] | Series: Earthforms | Includes bibliographical
   references and index.
Identifiers: LCCN 2024021061 (print) | LCCN 2024021062 (ebook) | ISBN
   9798892326216 (library binding) | ISBN 9798892327015 (paperback) | ISBN
   9798892326612 (ebook)
Subjects: LCSH: Sand dunes--Juvenile literature.
Classification: LCC GB631 .L64 2025 (print) | LCC GB631 (ebook) | DDC
   551.3/75--dc23/eng/20240609
LC record available at https://lccn.loc.gov/2024021061
LC ebook record available at https://lccn.loc.gov/202402106

Copyright © 2025 Bearport Publishing Company. All rights reserved. No part of this publication may be reproduced in whole or in part, stored in any retrieval system, or transmitted in any form or by any means, electronic, mechanical, photocopying, recording, or otherwise, without written permission from the publisher.

For more information, write to Bearport Publishing, 5357 Penn Avenue South, Minneapolis, MN 55419.

Contents

A Hill of Sand 4

Sleeping Bear Dunes 22

Glossary 23

Index 24

Read More 24

Learn More Online......................... 24

About the Author 24

A Hill of Sand

The wind blows in a hot **desert**.

Whoosh!

Sand piles up taller and taller.

It is a dune.

A dune is a pile of sand.

Some dunes are huge!

Others are small.

One side of a dune goes up like a hill.

The other side drops off.

It is **steep**.

This side looks like a **cliff**.

Dunes form all over the world.

Many are in deserts.

Others are on ocean and lake **shores**.

Some dunes even form underwater.

Strong wind makes dunes on land.

The wind carries sand a long way.

Then, the sand drops to the ground.

Big piles grow into dunes after a long time.

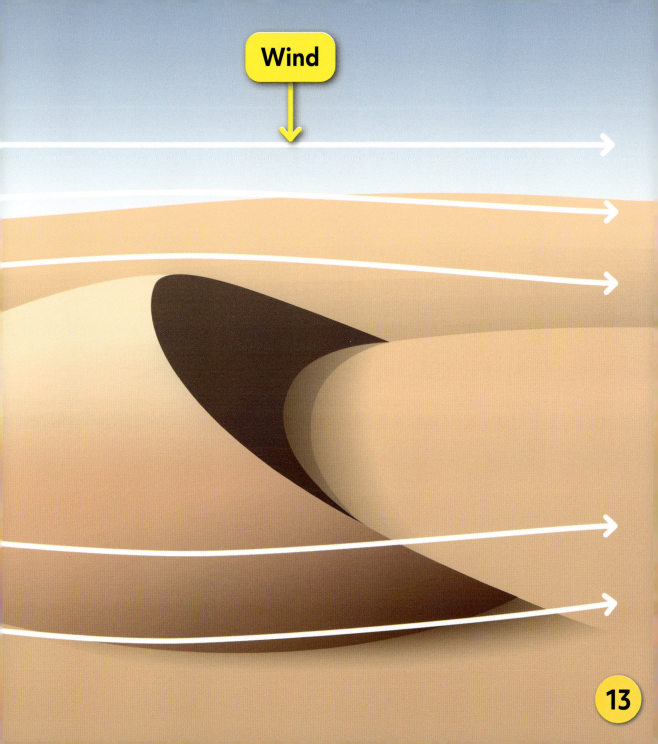

Under the water, waves push sand into piles.

Sometimes, they form dunes in long lines.

Other dunes look like sea stars on the ocean floor.

Many land animals live on dunes by the ocean.

Lizards dig homes in the sand.

Birds fly around looking for fish to eat.

Dunes help during storms. They block wind and waves. Water cannot get over tall dunes.

The big piles of sand keep people safe from floods.

Wind and waves are always moving.

That means dunes are always changing.

Are there any dunes near you?

Sleeping Bear Dunes

Sleeping Bear Dunes is one of the largest dune areas in the world.

The dunes are home to black bears and coyotes.

Some dunes are taller than a nine-story building!

The dunes were made during the last ice age thousands of years ago.

Glossary

cliff a high, steep surface of rock, earth, or ice

desert dry land with little or no rainfall

shores the lands along the edge of water

steep to drop off sharply

Index

desert 4, 10
floods 18
ocean 10, 14, 16
storms 18
water 10, 14, 18
wind 4, 12–13, 18, 20

Read More

Kinser, Heather Ferranti. *Nature Is a Sculptor: Weathering and Erosion.* Minneapolis: Lerner, 2024.

Twiddy, Robin. *Dunes (Coast Explorer).* New York: KidHaven Publishing, 2023.

Learn More Online

1. Go to **FactSurfer.com** or scan the QR code below.
2. Enter "**Earthforms Dunes**" into the search box.
3. Click on the cover of this book to see a list of websites.

About the Author

Martha London lives in Minnesota. She loves spending time outside.